D0586614

To: Josie

From: Nancy

lets laugh
together!!
enjoy

How Can I Miss Him... If He Won't Go Away?

By Nancy Rider Hunt

Introduction by Barbara Paulding

PETER PAUPER PRESS, INC.
White Plains, New York

To my family, who provided me with great material for this book, and especially to my mother, who loved olive sandwiches and a good laugh! She, however, was too classy and demure to have said these kinds of things.

Designed by Heather Zschock

Illustrations copyright © 2007 Olive Sandwiches, Inc.

Copyright © 2007
Peter Pauper Press, Inc.
202 Mamaroneck Avenue
White Plains, NY 10601
All rights reserved
ISBN 978-1-59359-873-0

Printed in China

7   6   5   4   3   2   1

Visit us at www.peterpauper.com

How Can I Miss Him...
If He Won't Go Away?

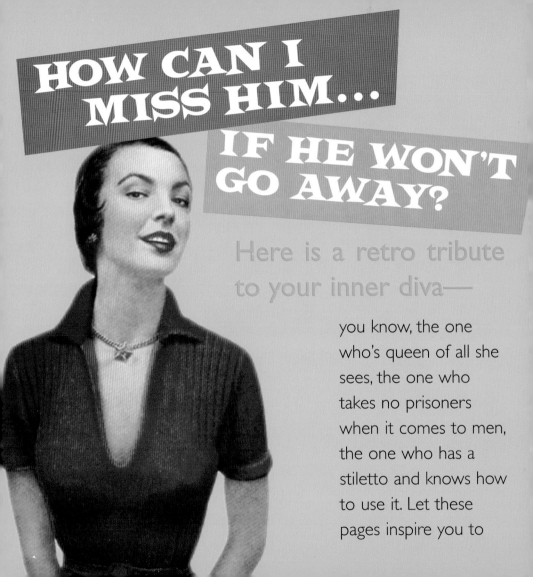

HOW CAN I MISS HIM...

IF HE WON'T GO AWAY?

Here is a retro tribute to your inner diva—

you know, the one who's queen of all she sees, the one who takes no prisoners when it comes to men, the one who has a stiletto and knows how to use it. Let these pages inspire you to add audacity to your attitude as you join the sisterhood whose motto, when it comes to fish and men, is "catch and release."

If you find yourself wondering if you should whip your guy into shape or just take him for a ride, join this madcap tour through the Land of Worthy Women, where men are welcome as long as they come fast, fun, and fully-funded. Like a woman, this little book makes up with wit and grit what it may lack in size, with a knowing nod to the fact that men *are* good for certain things.

Lest we be accused of reverse sexism, let us assure dear reader that "we have nothing against men, but we're looking for a cure."

Gardening, yoga, bubble baths, medication... and I still want to smack somebody!

The queen is not granting an audience today.

The more I see of men,
the more I like my
pet squirrel.

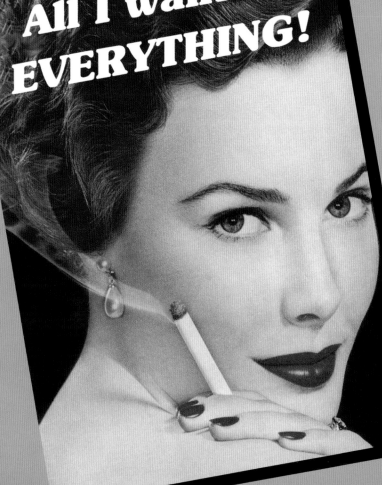

Have I told you lately that you bug me?

*I never met a man
I couldn't blame.*

Remember, darling, jewelry prevents headaches.

Back in my day, we hiked ten miles through the snow for sex & cigarettes!

She liked her men
fast, fun, and
fully funded!

When it came to
fish and men,
her motto was,
"catch and release."

It was SO cold,
I almost got
married!

she didn't need a man...
she had all the peckers
she could handle!

Some say men are just as sensitive as women...

but who really cares?

We have nothing against men, but we're looking for a cure!

I LIVE IN THE FAST LANE BUT I'M MARRIED TO A SPEED BUMP!

The problem with
"stud muffins"
is they don't
always rise!

A woman without a man is like a neck without pain.

Grow
your
own
dope ...

Plant
a man.

She wasn't crazy about either one, but she liked a little competition.

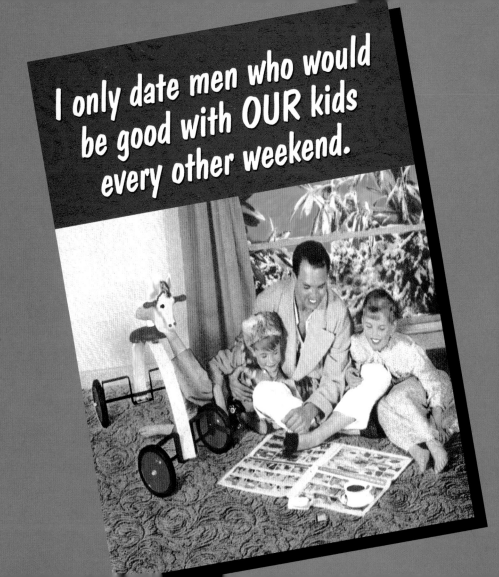

Just so you know, I renewed my backseat driver's license!

How can I miss him if he won't go away?

Never put off 'til tomorrow what your husband can do for you today!

FRIENDS ARE FOREVER! MEN ARE _WHATEVER_...

Naughty boy!
Go to my room!

I daydream about someone to "do me" AND the laundry!

After further study, he was history…